GREEN CRAFTS

Cool Crafts
with
Cardboard and
Wrapping Paper

by Jen Jones

green projects for Resourceful Kids

CAPSTONE PRESS
a capstone imprint

Snap Books are published by Capstone Press,
151 Good Counsel Drive, P.O. Box 669, Mankato, Minnesota 56002.
www.capstonepub.com

Books published by Capstone Press are manufactured with paper
containing at least 10 percent post-consumer waste.

Library of Congress Cataloging-in-Publication Data
Jones, Jen.
  Cool crafts with cardboard and wrapping paper : green projects for resourceful kids / by Jen Jones.
     p. cm.—(Snap. Green crafts)
  Includes bibliographical references and index.
  Summary: "Step-by-step instructions for crafts made from old cardboard and wrapping paper and
information about reusing and recycling"—Provided by publisher.
  ISBN 978-1-4296-4765-6 (library binding)
  1. Box craft—Juvenile literature. 2. Paper work—Juvenile literature. I. Title. II. Series.
  TT870.5.J66 2011
  745.54—dc22
                                    2010002277

Editorial Credits
Lori Shores, editor; Juliette Peters, designer; Sarah Schuette, photo stylist;
    Marcy Morin, project production; Laura Manthe, production specialist

Photo Credits
All photos by Capstone Studio/Karon Dubke except:
Jen Jones, 32
Shutterstock/Amy Johansson (chain link fence); Ian O'Hanlon (recycling stamp)

Essential content terms are **bold** and are defined at the bottom of the page
where they first appear.

Printed in the United States of America in North Mankato, Minnesota.
112010
006003R

Table of Contents

Introduction

Pretty presentation is a big part of what makes giving gifts fun. Wrapping paper is a great way to dress up packages. But boxes and wrappings are often tossed aside when we're happily enjoying our gifts. The bad news is that all the extra waste can really take its toll on the **environment**.

Luckily, going green doesn't have to mean a lifetime of plain-looking gifts. Cardboard and wrapping paper can be reused in new ways. From awesome accessories to darling display items, **recycled** crafts are gifts you can give yourself for free. Soon you'll be dreaming up more green gifts and making art all year long.

environment—the natural world of the land, water, and air

recycle—to make used items into new products

4

Go Metric!

It's easy to change measurements to metric! Just use this chart.

To change	into	multiply by
inches	centimeters	2.54
inches	millimeters	25.4
feet	meters	.305
yards	meters	.914

Did You Hear?

Each year, five million tons (4.5 million metric tons) of waste end up in landfills during the holidays. Wrapping paper and shopping bags make up about 80 percent of that trash. But the good news is that it's easy to cut down on packaging and gift wrap. Start by reusing gift bags and boxes. Then use recycled paper or newspaper comics to wrap gifts. Every little bit helps!

XXXX

landfill—an area where garbage is stacked and covered with dirt

Wrap It Up

You don't need a magic wand to turn everyday items into super-cute containers. All you need is some wrapping paper and a little imagination. Turn household items into cases for jewelry, photos, and more with the art of **decoupage**. With this project, even a used shoebox can become the sassiest storage around.

Here's what you need:
- scissors
- used wrapping paper
- cardboard box
  with lid
- old newspapers
- sponge brush
- decoupage glue

1

2

Step 1
Tear or cut used wrapping paper into small pieces. Place a cardboard box and lid on newspaper.

Step 2
Dip a sponge brush in decoupage glue. Apply a thin layer of glue to the back of one wrapping paper piece.

Step 3
Lay the piece flat on the box. Smooth out any wrinkles with your fingers.

Step 4
Cover the piece of wrapping paper and surrounding area with another thin layer of decoupage glue.

Step 5
Repeat steps 2 through 4 until the box and lid are covered with wrapping paper. Let dry for five minutes.

Step 6
Apply a thin layer of decoupage glue over the entire box and lid. Let dry completely before placing the lid on the box.

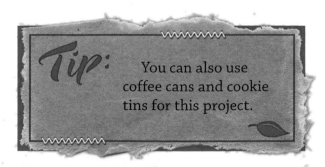

Tip: You can also use coffee cans and cookie tins for this project.

decoupage—the art of decorating a surface by pasting on pieces of paper and then covering the whole object with layers of glue

Bag Lady

Once upon a time you looked for a prize inside a cereal box. Now the box itself can be a lasting treasure! With a little paint and **matte** sealer, cereal boxes can turn into chic yet simple handbags. Even though it's not a canvas bag, this bag can be your artistic canvas. Paint on fun designs and show off your creativity!

Here's what you need:
- scissors
- cardboard cereal box
- pencil
- ruler
- old newspapers
- paintbrush
- acrylic paints
- clear matte sealer

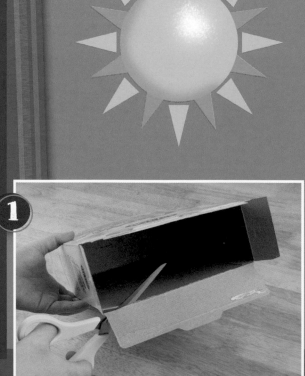

1

8

Step 1

Use scissors to remove the flaps at the top of a cereal box.

Step 2

On the front of the box, draw an oval about 3 inches wide by 1 inch tall. The oval should be centered and be about ¾ inch from the top edge. Cut out the oval. Repeat on other side of the box, making sure the two ovals match up.

Step 3

Place the box on top of old newspapers. Paint the outside of the box in a fun design. Let dry.

Step 4

Use a paintbrush to apply a thin layer of clear matte sealer to the whole box. Let dry.

Step 5

To make the bag easier to carry, fold the side edges to the inside. Make sharp folds about halfway down the bag.

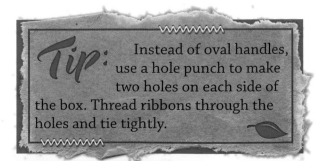

Tip: Instead of oval handles, use a hole punch to make two holes on each side of the box. Thread ribbons through the holes and tie tightly.

matte—not shiny

Stamp of Approval

Plain white envelopes are so yesterday. Nothing says, "Signed, sealed, delivered" like these charming **origami**-style envelopes! You'll find endless uses for these sassy sleeves. Use them for mailing notes, storing CDs, or sending homemade valentines.

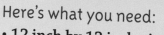

Here's what you need:
- 12 inch by 12 inch piece of thick used wrapping paper
- craft glue
- sticker

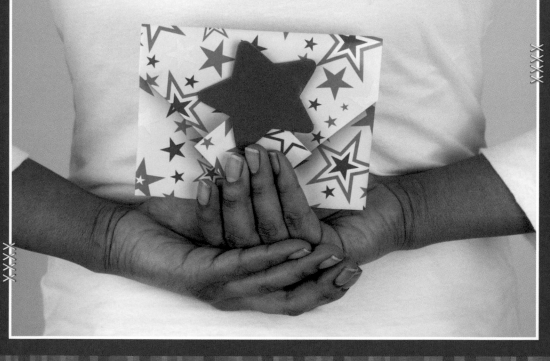

1

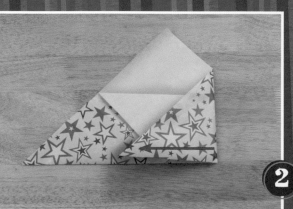

2

Step 1

Fold a square of wrapping paper in half diagonally to make a triangle. Then fold the top layer of the triangle down to meet the bottom center.

Step 2

Fold the right corner about ⅔ across the triangle. Glue down the bottom edge of this new triangle.

Step 3

Fold the left corner so the point meets the new right corner. Do not glue this triangle yet.

Step 4

Fold the new right corner flap back to the left corner. Glue down the bottom edge of the rest of the triangle made in step 3.

Step 5

Lift the little triangle you made in step 4 so it points straight up. Pull the sides of the triangle outward and flatten into a diamond shape.

Step 6

Once the glue is dry, fold the top of the envelope down to the bottom edge. Close the envelope by tucking the top flap into the diamond-shaped pocket. Secure with a sticker.

Tip: Be sure to use a white address label if sending regular mail. Also keep in mind that square envelopes may require extra postage.

origami—the Japanese art of paper folding

Pressed Paper

Odds are that hardly a day goes by that you don't use paper in dozens of ways. And while most paper is made by machines, making paper at home is easy and fun. Try your hand at recycling wrapping paper into paper **pulp**. Then form the pulp into a thick piece of paper to spruce up notes, cards, and more. The results are bound to be eco-tastic!

Here's what you need:
- 10 sheets of newspaper
- 4 old towels, about 12 inches by 8 inches each
- 1 cup used wrapping paper, torn into small pieces
- 4 cups hot water
- blender
- 9- by 13-inch pan
- 1 tablespoon white glue
- plastic spoon
- 12- by 8-inch piece of stiff screen
- rolling pin

Step 1

Prepare your workspace by placing five sheets of newspaper in a stack. Lay two old towels on top of the newspaper. Set two more towels and five more sheets of newspaper nearby.

Step 2

Combine wrapping paper and hot water in a blender and put on the lid. Let the paper soak for five minutes.

Step 3

Have an adult help you blend the mixture in short bursts on medium-high for 30 to 60 seconds.

Step 4

Pour the pulp into a 9x13 pan. Add white glue and stir with a plastic spoon.

pulp—a mixture of water and ground up paper or wood fibers

To finish this project, turn to the next page. ⇨

Step 5
Slide a screen into the bottom of the pan. Move the screen around to cover it evenly with pulp.

Step 6
Carefully remove the screen from the pan, holding it level as you lift it. Hold it over the pan to drain for 1 minute.

Step 7
Set the screen on the newspaper and towels you prepared in step 1. Make sure the pulp is on the top of the screen.

Step 8
Lay the remaining two towels over the screen and pulp. Lay the remaining sheets of newspaper over the towels.

Step 9

Roll a rolling pin over the top newspaper. Repeat several times to squeeze out as much water as you can.

Step 10

Remove the newspapers and towels from the top of the screen. Allow paper to dry on the screen for 24 hours.

Step 11 *(not pictured)*

Place any remaining pulp in the trash. Do not pour pulp down the drain as it can clog pipes.

Step 12

When the paper is completely dry, peel it away from the screen.

Tip: Add glitter or colored thread to the pulp for a more artistic look. Stir these items in after mixing the pulp in the blender.

Eco-Chic Frames

There's no need to spend a fortune on photo frames. You can make eco-chic ones at home. Capture those special moments with cute juice carton frames! Juicy **couture**, indeed.

Here's what you need:
- scissors
- 1-quart cardboard juice carton, clean and dry
- pencil
- ruler
- hole punch
- 2 straws
- glue
- 3- by 5-inch photo

1

2

Step 1

Cut one panel from an empty juice carton. Draw a rectangle measuring 2½ inches tall and 4½ inches wide in the middle of the panel. Carefully cut out the square.

Step 2

Make three evenly spaced accordion-style folds on the right side of the opening. With the side still folded, use a hole punch to make indents where holes need to be punched for the straws.

Step 3

Unfold the side and punch holes where the indents are.

Step 4 *(not pictured)*

Repeat steps 2 and 3 on the left side. Make sure the holes on the left are even with the holes on the right.

Step 5

Slide a straw through the holes at the top of the frame. Trim the straw if it sticks out too much on one side. Repeat on bottom.

Step 6

Apply a thin layer of glue around the edges on the front side of a photo. Glue the photo to the backside of the frame so the picture shows through the opening.

Tip: Feel free to think outside the box! Soda cases, milk cartons, and frozen dinner packages can also be used for a variety of fun frames.

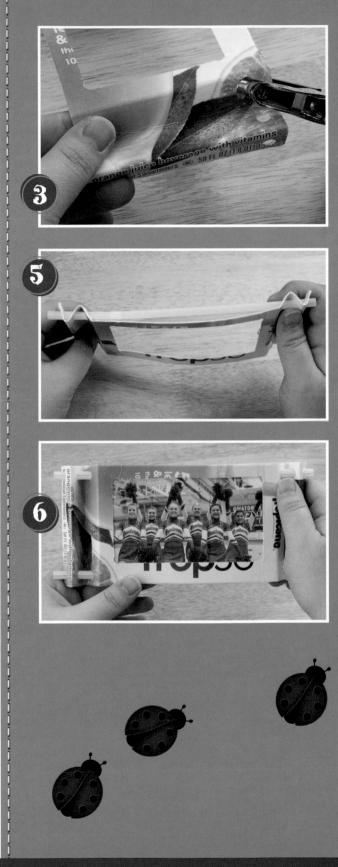

couture—something fashionable that is custom-made

Best Bow

Gift bags and bows can be almost as expensive as the gifts themselves. Do something good for the planet and your budget by creating your own gift wrap accessories. You can start with this neat little bow. Be resourceful and put the bow on the tote bag on page 8 for a great gift bag.

Here's what you need:
- scissors
- ruler
- thin cardboard, such as a cereal box
- 20 strips of used wrapping paper, 4 inches by 1 inch
- clear tape

Step 1 *(not pictured)*

Cut a 2-inch square of thin cardboard.

Step 2

Form a loop from one wrapping paper strip with the printed side facing outward. Use a small piece of clear tape to connect the ends of the loop.

Step 3

Use tape to attach the loop to one edge of the cardboard.

Step 4 *(not pictured)*

Continue making and adding loops around the cardboard square.

Step 5

Add more layers of loops to fill out the bow. Place the new loops between previous loops by taping them nearer to the center of the cardboard.

Step 6

Wrap a strip of wrapping paper around two fingers and cut to size. Tape this final loop in the center of the bow.

Tip: Make your bow more interesting by using different colors and designs for the loops.

Pinned Up

From to-do lists to photos, your desk can get messy fast. Give your work space a marvelous makeover with a one-of-a-kind organizer. This do-it-yourself bulletin board keeps all your VIP stuff in one place. Who knew staying tidy could be so cool?

Here's what you need:
- scissors
- ruler
- old T-shirt
- 10- by 15-inch piece of thick cardboard
- glue gun and hot glue
- ½-inch wide ribbon, 6 feet
- thumbtacks

Step 1
Cut an 11- by 16-inch rectangle from the front or back of an old T-shirt.

Step 2
Center the fabric on the cardboard and wrap it tightly around to the back. Hot glue the fabric edges to the backside of the cardboard.

Step 3
Cut ribbon into four 9-inch strips and two 18-inch strips. Arrange strips in a crisscross pattern on the front of the bulletin board. Use thumbtacks to hold the ribbons in place where they cross.

Step 4
Turn the board over. Pull the end of one ribbon tight to the back of the board and hot glue in place. Repeat with both ends of all ribbons.

Step 5
Use thumbtacks to attach to-do lists and other items to the board. Tuck photos behind ribbons.

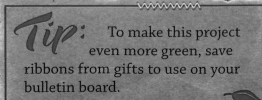

Tip: To make this project even more green, save ribbons from gifts to use on your bulletin board.

Check It Out

Quicker than you can say "king me," you'll be the queen of this easy checkerboard. Whether you prefer one-on-one fun or tourney play, this project will supply hours of game-playing glee. Invite the girls over for game night. Be sure to order a pizza so you can make another checkerboard!

Here's what you need:

- **medium or large pizza box, clean**
- **newspaper**
- **spray paint, white**
- **ruler**
- **pencil**
- **paintbrush**
- **acrylic paints**
- **permanent marker, black**
- **high gloss spray sealer**
- **24 plastic bottle caps, 12 each of two colors**

Step 1
Place a pizza box on newspapers outside. Spray paint the pizza box inside and outside with white paint. Let dry.

Step 2
Use a ruler and pencil to draw eight vertical rows about 1½ inches wide on top of the pizza box. Then draw eight horizontal rows about 1 ½ inches wide. When you are done, you should have 64 evenly sized squares.

Step 3
Use any color to paint a border around the outside of the box. Leave the large center square white.

Step 4
In the large center square, carefully paint every other inside square any color. Let dry.

Step 5
Use a ruler and a permanent marker to trace the lines on the top of the box.

Step 6
Take the box outside and place it on newspaper. Spray the box with high gloss sealer. Let dry.

Step 7 *(not pictured)*
Use bottle caps as checkers. Store them inside the box when not in use.

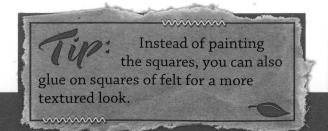

Tip: Instead of painting the squares, you can also glue on squares of felt for a more textured look.

Off the Cuff

Wrap your wrist in this **eco-friendly** beaded cuff! With beads made out of used wrapping paper, this accessory is a gift that keeps on giving. Soon you'll see that going green has never been so stylish.

Here's what you need:
- ruler
- scissors
- used wrapping paper
- glue stick
- round toothpicks
- craft foam
- clear nail polish
- elastic string,
    about 9 feet long

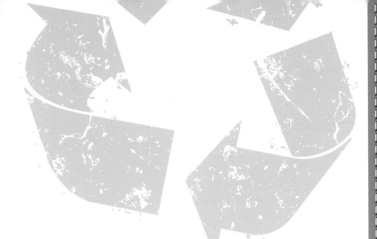

Step 1
Measure and cut an 10-inch long by 2-inch wide triangle from wrapping paper.

Step 2
Rub a glue stick down the white side of the triangle.

Step 3
Center the toothpick on the wide end of the triangle.

Step 4
Wind the rest of the triangle tightly around the toothpick with the printed side facing outward. Glue the end down.

eco-friendly—causing minimal or no harm to the environment

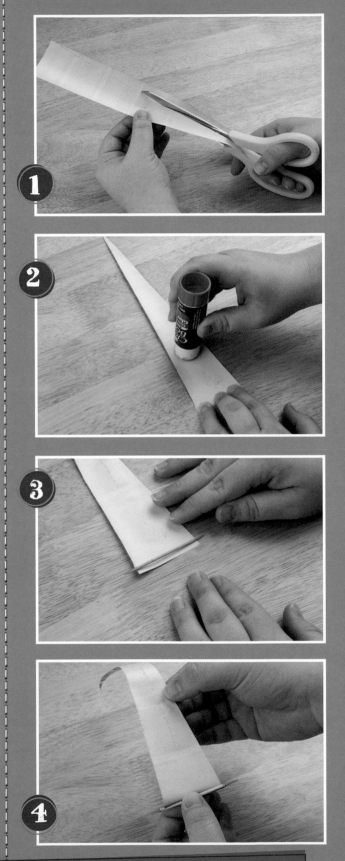

To finish this project, turn to the next page. ⇨

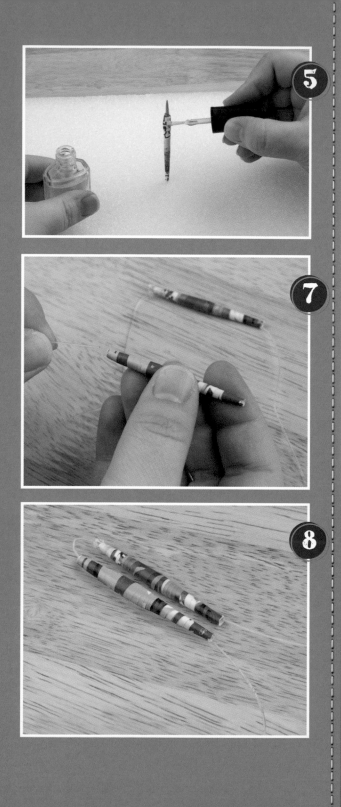

Step 5

Stick the end of the toothpick into a piece of craft foam. Apply two coats of clear nail polish to the paper bead. Avoid getting nail polish on the toothpick. Let dry.

Step 6 *(not pictured)*

Repeat steps 1 through 5 until you have 25 to 30 beads. Remove the toothpicks from inside the paper beads.

Step 7

Thread a piece of elastic string through one bead. Center the bead in the middle of the string. Thread the left end of the string through a second bead.

Step 8

Position the bead so that it lays close to the first bead. You should have both ends of the string on the right side.

XXXX

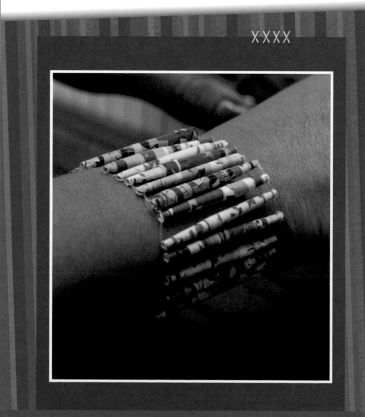

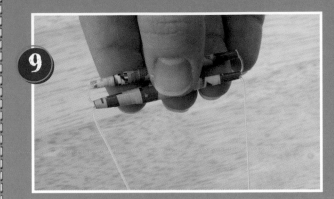

Step 9

Thread the end of the string from the first bead through the second bead. You will have one end of the string on either side of the second bead.

Step 10

Continue adding beads one at a time as in steps 7 through 9. Pull the ends tight to keep the beads laying together flat.

Step 11

When the bracelet is long enough to wrap around your wrist, thread one end of the string through the first bead. Tie both ends together tightly in a knot. Snip off any extra string.

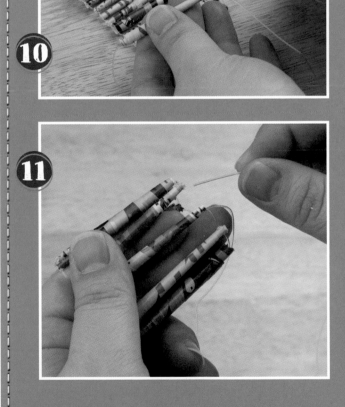

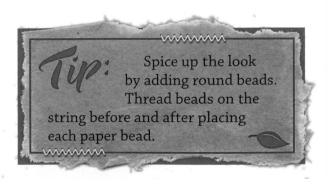

Tip: Spice up the look by adding round beads. Thread beads on the string before and after placing each paper bead.

Green Crafting Facts

Birthdays and holidays and graduations, oh my! Between all the special occasions in a year, it's easy to gather a bunch of gift bags from others. Be sure to save them in a special place for your own gift-giving needs.

Next time you get a cardboard package in the mail, don't toss it away! Save the box for future mailings or take it to a nearby recycling center.

Everyone loves greeting cards, but all that paper can add up. Save some trees by sending cards made of recycled content. Or even better, reuse materials to make your own!

Cardboard can also be used to spruce up your yard. Spread a few layers of cardboard around plants in your garden or flower bed. The cardboard will be hidden by the leaves and help control weeds.

Glossary

couture (koo-TUR)—something fashionable that is custom-made

decoupage (day-koo-PAHZH)—the art of decorating a surface by pasting on pieces of paper and then covering the whole object with layers of glue

eco-friendly (EE-koh-frend-lee)—causing minimal or no harm to the environment; eco-friendly is short for ecologically friendly

environment (in-VY-ruhn-muhnt)—the natural world of the land, water, and air

landfill (LAND-fill)—an area where garbage is stacked and covered with dirt

matte (MAT)—not shiny

origami (or-uh-GAH-mee)—the Japanese art of paper folding

pulp (PUHLP)—a mixture of water and ground up paper or wood fibers

recycle (ree-SYE-kuhl)—to make used items into new products

Read More

Meinking, Mary. *Easy Origami.* Origami. Mankato, Minn.: Capstone Press, 2009.

Monaghan, Kimberly. *Organic Crafts: 75 Earth-friendly Art Activities.* Chicago: Chicago Review Press, 2007.

Sirrine, Carol. *Cool Crafts with Old Wrappers, Cans, and Bottles: Green Projects for Resourceful Kids.* Green Crafts. Mankato, Minn.: Capstone Press, 2010.

Internet Sites

FactHound offers a safe, fun way to find Internet sites related to this book. All of the sites on FactHound have been researched by our staff.

Here's all you do:

Visit *www.facthound.com*

Type in this code: 9781429647656

Index

About the Author

A Midwesterner-turned-California girl, Jen Jones loves to be in nature and is proud to be part of any project that makes our world a greener place! Jen is a Los Angeles-based writer who has authored more than 35 books for Capstone Press. Her stories have been published in magazines such as *American Cheerleader, Dance Spirit, Ohio Today,* and *Pilates Style.* She has also written for E! Online, MSN, and PBS Kids, as well as being a Web site producer for major talk shows such as *The Jenny Jones Show, The Sharon Osbourne Show,* and *The Larry Elder Show.* Jen is a member of the Society of Children's Book Writers and Illustrators.